Guid ... on

MW01675875

YOUTH MINISTRIES

Ministries for, by, and with youth

By Terry Carty and Susan Hay
General Board of Discipleship

YOUTH MINISTRIES

This book is printed on acid-free paper.

ISBN 0-687-00270-2

MANUFACTURED IN THE UNITED STATES OF AMERICA

CONTENTS

Our Identity, Call, and Mission

You are so important to the life of the Christian church! You have consented to be among a great and long line of people who have shared the faith and led others in the work of Jesus Christ. We have the church only because over the millennia people like you have caught the vision of God's kingdom and have claimed a place in the faith community to extend God's love to others. You have been called and have committed your unique passions, gifts, and abilities in a position of leadership, and this guide will help you understand some of the elements of that ministry and how it fits within the mission of your church and of The United Methodist Church.

"The mission of the Church is to make disciples of Jesus Christ. Local churches provide the most significant arena through which disciple-making occurs" (*The Book of Discipline of The United Methodist Church, 2004,* ¶120). The church is not only local but also global, and it is for everyone. Our church has an organizational structure through which we work, but it is a living organism as well. Each person is called to ministry by virtue of his or her baptism, and that ministry takes place in all aspects of daily life, not just within the walls of the church. Our *Book of Discipline* describes our mission to proclaim the gospel and to welcome people into the body of Christ, to lead people to a commitment to God through Jesus Christ, to nurture them in Christian living by various means of grace, and to send them into the world as agents of Jesus Christ (¶121). Thus, through you—and many other Christians—this very relational mission continues. (The *Discipline* explains the ministry of all Christians and the essence of servant ministry and leadership in ¶¶125–137.)

Essential Leadership Functions

Five functions of leadership are essential to strengthen and support the ministry of the church: identifying and supporting leaders as spiritual leaders, discovering current reality, naming shared vision, developing action plans, and monitoring the journey. This Guideline will help you identify these elements and set a course for ministry.

Lead in the Spirit

Each leader is a spiritual leader and has the opportunity to model spiritual maturity and discipline. John Wesley referred to the disciplines that cultivate a relationship with God as the "means of grace" and suggested several means: prayer, Bible study, fasting, public and private worship, Christian conversation, and acts of mercy. Local church leaders are strongly encouraged to identify their own spiritual practices, cultivate new ones as they grow in their own faith, and model and encourage these practices among their ministry team participants.

Discover Current Reality

"The way things are" is your current reality. How you organize, who does what, how bills get paid and plans get made are all building blocks of your current reality. Spend time with people who have been in this ministry and with your committee members to assess their view of how things are. Use "Christian conversation," one of the means of grace, not only to talk to others openly about their understanding of current reality but also to listen for the voice of God regarding your area of ministry.

Name Shared Vision

"The way things are" is only a prelude to "the way you want things to be." When the church is truly of God, it is the way God would envision it to be. Spend time with your committee and with other leaders in the church to discern the best and most faithful future you can imagine. How can you together identify your role and place in a faithful community that extends itself in its fourfold mission of reaching out and receiving people in the name of God, relating people to God, nurturing them in Christ and Christian living, and sending them forth as ministers into the world? Examine your committee's role and its place in that big picture and try to see yourselves as God's agents of grace and love.

Develop Action Plans

How do you get from here (your current reality) to there (your shared vision)? As a leader, one of your tasks is to hold in view both what is and what is hoped for so that you can build bridges to the future. These bridges are the interim goals and the action plans needed to accomplish the goals that will make your vision a reality. Remember that God may open up many (or different) avenues to that future, so be flexible and open to setting new goals and accepting new challenges. Action plans that describe how to meet interim goals should be specific, measurable, and attainable. While it is faithful to allow for the wondrous work of God in setting out bold plans, balance that boldness with realism. You and your committee will find information and tips here on developing and implementing the shared vision, the goals toward that vision, and the specific action plans that will accomplish the goals.

Monitor the Journey

A fifth responsibility of leaders is to keep an eye on how things are going. Setbacks will surely occur, but effective leaders keep moving toward their envisioned future. Not only will you monitor the progress of your committee's action plans to a faithful future but you will also be called to evaluate them in light of the ministry of the rest of the church. Immerse yourself and your plans in God's love and care. Voices from the congregation (both pro and con) may be the nudging of God to shift direction, rethink or plan, or move ahead boldly and without fear. Faithful leaders are attentive to the discernment of the congregation and to the heart of God in fulfilling the mission of the church.

Welcome to Ministry By, With and For Youth

Welcome to the world of ministry by, with, and for youth—a place of joys, challenges, frustrations, meaningful conversations, and new insights about God! You have been selected to lead youth ministry in your congregation. This job should excite you with hope as you find ways for God's love to be shared among the youth in your congregation and community, a job that is exciting, rewarding, and meaningful.

Remember your own adolescence. Think back to your adolescent memories of the church. Was it a friendly place? Did you feel loved? Can you recall special people during these years who were there for you? special events at your church? What do you remember learning about God? about Jesus? the Holy Spirit? As an adolescent, what were your expectations of the adults in the youth ministry program? If you weren't active in a youth ministry program during your adolescent years, what memories do you want to provide for youth?

Think of your church today. Do youth find it a friendly place? Do the adults who work with the youth truly care for and love this age? Are there opportunities for youth and their families to share in the ministry and grow in their faith? Are youth given opportunities to share in the total life and worship of the congregation? Are there a variety of discipling experiences in which youth can participate? Is there intentional outreach to youth in the community? Are youth given an opportunity to plan and lead their own activities?

Youth Ministries has been written to prepare you as a leader in youth ministry in your local church setting. It doesn't matter what size your church is or even how you are structured. This Guideline has been designed to help you focus on The United Methodist Church's commitment to a ministry by, with, and for youth. It contains ideas and suggestions to help you create a church where youth experience God's love, feel included in the life of the congregation, and have opportunities to grow in their faith.

Youth ministry is a process, not a program, by which youth are led to a deeper relationship with Christ and a deeper commitment to the work of the church in the world. Youth ministry is a process that moves all who participate in it from just participation to opportunities for transformation.

Start at the Beginning

Let's make certain we understand exactly who and what we are talking about when we say *youth* and *youth ministry*. Youth ministry is anything the church does that is by, with, and for youth. That definition means, then, that ushering, mission projects, reading Scripture in worship, child care, and even visiting prospective members are youth ministry if they involve youth.

"The term *youth ministries* is an inclusive title, encompassing all the concerns of the Church and all activities by, with, and for youth. The youth ministries of The United Methodist Church shall include all persons from approximately twelve through eighteen years of age (generally persons in the seventh grade through the twelfth grade, taking into account the grouping of youth in the public schools), who are currently or potentially associated with the church or any of its activities. Youth who are members of the church have all the rights and responsibilities of church membership except voting on matters prohibited by state law" (*The Book of Discipline of The United Methodist Church,* ¶256.2).

Youth ministry may include people who are younger than seventh grade because of the way their schools group grades together or because they need to involve more age groups in order to have enough youth for activities. Youth ministry also focuses on people who are currently or potentially associated with the church or any of its activities. Therefore, it should include youth who are not members of your church— those who play on your youth basketball team or come to the Valentine dance or live in your neighborhood.

Getting Started

If you are an adult who feels comfortable with youth, is excited about working with youth, likes the idea of being *in* ministry *with* young people, and sees this as an opportunity to share your faith journey with young people in an atmosphere of acceptance and unconditional love, then perhaps God is calling you to work with young people as coordinator of youth ministry.

What Is My Job as Coordinator of Youth Ministry?

You are the layperson in the congregation who holds the "big picture" of the congregation's ministries with youth. The congregation looks to you for resources, understanding, and direction in its ministries with youth. Depending upon the size of the congregation, your position can become quite demanding. You will work together with your church's pastor, staff, and others who have a passion and calling to be in ministry with youth to promote the development of a comprehensive approach to youth ministry in your church. If you are in a church that has a youth staff person, it is important that you spend time together looking at the "big picture" of youth ministry in your congregation and how the work will be delegated and accomplished between you. It is extremely important in staffing situations that each of you clearly understands how you will be working together and who is responsible for what in the overall ministry by, with, and for youth.

Responsibilities: Coordinator of Youth Ministry

According to the *Book of Discipline* (¶256.2), you will:

- recommend to the church council your suggestions for the activities, program emphases, and settings for youth
- use available resources and means to inform youth concerning the Youth Service Fund (see page 16) and cultivate its support
- challenge youth to assume their financial responsibilities in connection with the total program and budget of the local church
- be accountable to the charge conference through the church council.

Your specific responsibilities will probably include:

- helping your congregation to be aware of the hopes, concerns, and needs of youth in your community in order to determine how to serve them as Christian disciples and good neighbors
- helping others understand their roles in ministry with youth. These others include Sunday school teachers, adult workers with a youth group, youth who are leaders, parents, congregation members, and so on. For more about these roles in ministry, see the following chapters of this Guidelines or consult the *United Methodist Youth Handbook,* by Micheal Selleck (see Resources).
- keeping your congregation focused on the primary task of youth ministry (see pages 11-12)
- encouraging inclusion of youth in the goals of the congregation
- encouraging the inclusion of youth in decision-making committees of the congregation
- supporting and guiding the work of a council on youth ministry (see pages 17-20)
- helping plan and carry out a varied and wide-ranging program with youth, which includes settings for worship, study, fellowship, and service

- ensuring that every group related to ministry with youth is organized for youth and adult participation in decisions related to its ongoing life
- being aware of resources for developing programs for youth and participating in training experiences
- being a liaison with organizations, people, and resources that relate to youth and youth ministry.

Your responsibilities may sometimes include:

- serving as convener of a council on youth ministry or serve as co-convening the council with a youth and the coordinator
- organizing parents and other congregational members in youth ministry support activities (meals, transportation, fundraising, and so on)
- mentoring youth as they emerge as leaders
- coordinating church school curriculum and recruiting teachers
- keeping records of youth participation and managing youth ministry funds (where there is a separate account)
- serving on committees as needed (for example, age-level council, staff/pastor-parish committee, and other appropriate committees and task forces created by your congregation).

So Many Things to Do!

With so many things to do as coordinator of youth ministry you may be asking, *What am I to do first?* Try using the checklist below to organize your initial tasks:

Pray to God for guidance. Sense God's closeness as you embark on this new, exciting ministry. Ask God to open your mind to learning and your heart to loving. Pray for the youth and their families in your congregation and in your community. You will be a spiritual leader for your congregation in youth ministry.

Collect information by:

- *Listening.* What words do you hear from parents? from the adults working with youth? from the congregation? from church leaders? from the minister and staff? from youth regarding your youth ministry?
- *Seeking out youth to talk with and listen to.* Ask the youth of your congregation (those who are active *and* those who are not!) to tell you about themselves—their struggles, hopes, dreams, daily lives, fears, and desires. This conversation may take time to develop, as many youth believe that most adults do not want to listen to them. Be patient. As youth discover your will-

ingness to be open, receptive, and caring, they will share more of their life stories, narratives rich in meaning and full of faith.

- *Talking to other adults who work with youth.* Discuss the tasks of the youth coordinator with other adults who have worked extensively with youth. Your search for these persons may take you to other local church communities. Recognize the importance of developing new relationships with other adults who are engaged in youth ministry. These persons can be exciting centers of support, strength, ideas, and guidance. To be sure, spend time talking with the parents of your youth; these adult workers with youth have much wisdom to share!
- *Talking with the pastor and other church staff.* Ask your pastor, Christian educator, church musician, or other staff members who work with youth to share their experiences, insights, resources, and suggestions. They probably can show you some printed resource materials that you will find helpful in designing sessions, teaching other adults about the diversity of adolescence, and inviting youth to participate in the life of the church.

Develop a team of adult workers with youth. If there are already adults in place, call an initial meeting of all adults working with youth. Spend time sharing experiences, telling stories, and developing a sense of community. Pray and study Scripture with one another. If there are no adults already in place, seek out adults who are caring, confident, competent, committed to young people, and who seek to answer the question, "How may I be present with these young persons in an authentic, vulnerable, compassionate, and committed way?" Above all, don't do youth ministry alone! A team approach allows for you to be supported as the coordinator, not the sole voice of youth ministry.

Develop a leadership team that includes both adult workers and youth. Begin planning a comprehensive approach to youth ministry using the primary task of youth ministry. Make sure that your approach promotes ministries in the following areas:

- *Teaching and learning*. Where will youth learn the stories of the faith? How will youth learn to be teachers of the faith?
- *Community life.* Are youth invited into every aspect of the life of the congregation? Do they serve on all church committees? Do they know what it feels like to belong to a loving community of faith?
- *Worship.* Do youth regularly participate as leaders during Sunday morning worship? Do most youth gatherings have a time for worship, prayer, and celebration?
- *Outreach.* Do youth possess an active role in serving others, proclaiming the gospel of Jesus Christ, and seeking to make their community and world more loving and just?

The Primary Task of Youth Ministry

To put it simply, the primary task of The United Methodist Church is to see youth thriving in the world as faithful disciples. Youth ministry in The United Methodist Church can help youth follow Jesus by connecting youth practices and disciplines of the faith.

"There shall be a comprehensive approach to development and implementation of youth ministry programming at all levels of the Church. The comprehensive approach is based on the understanding of the primary task of youth ministry: to love youth where they are, to encourage them in developing their relationship to God, to provide them with opportunities for nurture and growth, and to challenge them to respond to God's call to serve in their communities" (*Book of Discipline,* ¶1119.2).

There are many ministries that fit the primary task of youth ministry. You will need to examine the resources of your community and congregation to decide what will be best for the youth in your area. Some examples that have worked for others include:

To Love Youth Where They Are—

- Basketball league (or other sports)
- May Day picnic in the park
- Ski trip (or other adventures)
- Periodic recreational-oriented fellowship opportunities for bringing unchurched friends
- Panel discussion of careers
- Lock-in at the church
- Visits by pastor and adult youth workers to students during lunch at school or attend students' ball games

To Encourage Youth in Developing Their Relationship to God—

- Church worship services
- Fellowship sessions about who God is and other fundamentals of faith
- Retreats focusing on God's creation
- Mission trips
- Involvement with adults who live out and can talk about their faith

- Sunday school and Fellowship sessions that help youth know how to tell others about their faith; how to describe God
- District and conference retreats
- Youth choirs that have the opportunity to sing during worship services

To Provide Opportunities to Nurture and Grow in their Faith—

- Youth leadership in worship services
- Sunday school sessions about famous and/or little known people of faith
- Fellowship sessions about the history and structure of The United Methodist Church
- Sharing groups based upon everyday experiences
- Good, communicating relationships between younger youth and older youth, and between youth and adults (especially mentoring ministries)
- An overall leadership attitude that it is OK for a youth to be at any stage within the faith-development process
- Discovery sessions about mission possibilities for individuals (and possibly ministry careers)
- Spiritual-discipline retreats (silence, fasting, prayer, journaling, spiritual creativity)
- Leadership positions for youth in youth ministry and service on committees within the local church

To Challenge Youth to Respond to God's Call Through—

- One-on-one ministries specially tailored to youth needs
- Specialized training in small groups (faith sharing, ministry skills, leadership skills, mission skills)
- Assistance for youth in finding personal mission opportunities
- Reflection groups (reflect upon mission or ministry experiences)
- Leadership positions for youth in the local church and beyond.

Where Youth Ministry Happens

Youth ministry can happen anywhere there are youth. Most youth ministry occurs in one-on-one connections between people. But there are some structures within United Methodist churches that make organized youth ministry possible.

Worship Services

The primary entry point for people into the life of the church is the worship service. The main worship services at a church are a focal point of the ministry effort of the church and should, therefore, in their design address the concerns and needs of youth.

Although it is good to involve youth in the leadership of worship (reading Scripture, leading responses and prayers, and so on), this does not ensure that the service speaks to youth needs. It is important that youth are involved in planning for worship, so their understanding of true worship can be considered. Meetings of youth with the pastor to discuss the meaning and design of worship can be helpful to pastor and youth alike. Including one or two youth on the worship committee can provide opportunities for both input and learning.

Church School and Sunday School

Almost every church has a church school ministry on Sunday mornings. This is a prime time to teach youth about faith.

Make the most of the church school hour by deciding exactly what you want to accomplish in the time. It is probably the best time to teach the Bible or religious history. It may be a good time for a pastor's faith and membership enhancement class. When a goal is set for church school teaching, stick to it.

There is plenty of good church school curriculum material available from a variety of publishing companies, but The United Methodist Publishing House provides the only curriculum that is prepared especially for United Methodist youth. It is biblically based, Wesleyan in theology, and United Methodist in its world view.

Fellowship Setting (formerly known as UMYF)

The Fellowship setting is more than just an evening of food, fellowship, and fun. It is one of the primary settings where youth can take seriously their journeys of faith: to encounter the living Christ. Through building relationships, asking questions, worshiping God, and transforming lives, youth in this setting can learn what it means to be the church.

The Fellowship experience stands as one of the most significant influences available to local church youth. As youth grow from junior high to senior high to young adults, those who are involved in this aspect of a youth ministry program learn to live lives of faith, mission, and Christian values as they spend time together with other youth.

The Fellowship setting usually meets at least once a week, for many groups, on Sunday evening. The format varies, but often includes a light meal, a recreation time, and a session about some facet of Christian living. The session time can be designed and led by an adult leader, a youth leader, or a combined team. It can be an activity leading to a discussion, or it can be a guest speaker followed by a question-answer time. It can be a field trip, or it can be a worship service. Most sessions end with a closing worship time or at least the traditional UMYF benediction.

Many Fellowship settings are the core of a complete system of youth ministry that also includes mission trips, service projects, recreational activities, Bible studies, camping trips, special interest studies, and mentoring arrangements. When this is the case, it is important that there is planning and coordination of activities.

NOTE: It is Christian worship and mission that sets a Christian youth group apart from social or service clubs. These are crucial to any United Methodist Youth Ministry setting.

The UMYF Benediction

The UMYF benediction as a closing ritual for youth groups has been a tradition followed in many congregations of our denomination for many years. Group members stand in a circle, crossing their right arms over their left arms and then joining hands. Some groups bow their heads and close their eyes, while others keep their eyes open and look around the circle at each person.

In unison (often in response to the first seven words offered by a leader) the UMYF says: "The LORD bless you and keep you: The LORD make his face to shine upon you, and be gracious to you: The LORD lift up his countenance upon you, and give you peace" (Numbers 6:24-26, RSV). Some groups add: "Amen."

Then while continuing to hold hands and lifting their right arms over their heads, the entire group turns to their right to face outward into the world.

Hearing the Voice of God

Kevin is in the tenth grade. While occasionally teased for his lanky looks, his peers think he is ambitious and outgoing. He joined the Fellowship group last year when several of his friends kept inviting him to attend. Since then, Kevin has felt affirmed for his leadership abilities. Just elected as a representative to the council on youth ministry, he has been talking with Fellowship members about session ideas, worship opportunities, and potential service projects in their town. When asked about "hearing the voice of God," Kevin quickly replies, "The hearing is in the doing. I feel God when I make a difference in the lives of others."

Study Groups

Fellowship settings and Sunday school generally speak to the needs of the majority of the youth. Special study groups offer small-group settings in which youth disciples can work through details of faith development. Bible studies are always a good choice for study groups. Studies can be designed for youth of different ages and to address different issues. A study group for the purpose of training youth for leadership will be extremely helpful.

Many Bible study resources are available commercially. DISCIPLE*: Becoming Disciples through Bible Study, Youth Edition* (information and training available through the DISCIPLE Office at The United Methodist Publishing House) is a study opportunity for advanced young disciples.

The *Book of Discipline* recommends a pastor's class on faith development for senior highs. Such a class should emphasize the doctrines, nature, and mission of The United Methodist Church and lead to continued growth in the knowledge, grace, and service of Christ. Many junior highs have missed the opportunity to participate in confirmation training; be sure to include this in planning for the younger youth.

Covenant Discipleship groups (sometimes called "Branch Groups") have been designed for youth by the General Board of Discipleship of The United Methodist Church. These groups are an adaptation of John Wesley's class meetings and help youth in their efforts to lead disciplined Christian lives.

Mission Projects

It is sometimes easier for youth to enter the mission field through organizations like Sierra Service Project, Mountain T.O.P., or Camp Aldersgate. Local churches can involve youth in Volunteers in Mission projects or Habitat for Humanity. Mission projects should offer youth a place to become involved, and they should help youth consider a lifestyle of helping other people.

After "learning the ropes," youth groups should begin to seek out mission opportunities on their own. Both The United Methodist General Board of Discipleship and General Board of Global Ministries have developed Web sites that feature many mission opportunities as a resource for youth groups.

Other Involvement in the Church

There are many other ministry settings within and beyond the local church that can meet the specific needs of individual youth. Pastors, church professionals, adult youth workers, and other youth can help individuals find the ministries they need. Possibilities include:

- United Methodist Women, United Methodist Men
- boards, councils, committees of the local church
- the larger Church: district, conference, jurisdiction, general UMC, interdenominational youth and adult ministry opportunities.

Through Christian Practices and Disciplines

Practice, and cultivating discipline to engage in the Christian practices, are vital in helping youth to develop a relationship with God and to mature in their faith life and faith community. Christian practices include:

- worshiping God together
- telling the Christian story to one another
- interpreting Scripture in the midst of a confusing world
- praying
- suffering with and for each other
- providing hospitality and practicing tolerance
- struggling together to form a community
- working together to create patterns and relationships that build sustainable lifestyles for the future
- in the pattern of John Wesley, practicing acts of piety and compassion.

Youth Service Fund

The Youth Service Fund (YSF) is money that is given by youth, administered by youth, and used to serve youth. YSF is more than simply raising money, however. YSF is a commitment made by United Methodist youth to serve those in need—in their own communities, across the United States, and around the world. YSF is the only authorized United Methodist fund directly related to youth. It is the only fund over which youth have primary administrative control. It truly can be considered second-mile giving because it does not replace a young person's responsibility for giving to his or her local church. *The YSF works like this:*

1. Money is raised by youth in the church.
2. The money is sent from the church to the treasurer of the annual conference. Your pastor can supply the name and address.
3. Seventy percent of the money is retained in the annual conference: one-third goes to projects within the conference; one-third goes to projects outside the conference; one-third is used for YSF education and administration. Youth representatives of the Conference Council on Youth Ministries (or equivalent structure) decide how grant requests will be funded.
4. Thirty percent is sent to the Division on Ministries With Young People of the General Board of Discipleship to support projects across the world. At least 70 percent of this amount goes to projects selected by the Projects Review Committee of the Steering Committee. The balance is used for resource promotion and interpretation.

The Council on Youth Ministry

The function of the council on youth ministry is to see that the best possible youth ministry is offered to the youth of your church. This council oversees all youth ministry of the congregation and advocates for ministry with youth in the total life of the church. These are important and necessary tasks for your church, regardless of its size.

Smaller churches may wish to do this task by occasionally calling together youth and adult leaders of various youth activities of the church. With six to twelve youth in the total church membership, you can function as a unit to plan, implement, and evaluate all aspects of your ministry with youth. Keep procedures flexible and rotate or share responsibilities. As you reach out to others and your group becomes larger, you will need to develop additional structures to meet your changing needs. Larger churches, therefore, usually find it very beneficial to establish a council on youth ministry to make sure all parts of youth ministry are cared for.

Often the council in a larger church does not do detailed planning for the component groups within youth ministry. Junior high and senior high fellowship settings, the church-school classes, and other groups for youth (youth choir, study groups, cell groups, mission groups) have their own ongoing planning groups and designated leaders. These all are usually accountable to and represented on the council.

Membership on the council should include both youth and adults, preferably at least two youth for every adult. The *Discipline* requires that at least one-half of the membership be youth. Youth members could include representatives from Sunday school; the junior and senior high Fellowship settings; other groups such as youth choir and so forth; and at-large members who serve as representatives to the district, conference, or beyond.

Adult members (while keeping the 2:1 ratio) could include the coordinator of youth ministry, the pastor or employed youth worker, a Sunday school teacher, an adult counselor, the coordinator of Scouting, a representative from the church council, and a parent.

Responsibilities of the Council on Youth Ministry

The *Book of Discipline* (¶256.2c) states that there may be a council on youth ministry, with the coordinator of youth ministry, that will recommend to the church council activities, program emphases, and settings for youth and that will use available resources and means to inform youth concerning the Youth Service Fund and to cultivate its support.

Responsibilities that are usually included are:

- evaluating the youth ministry and making recommendations so that present and future needs of youth are addressed (such as addition of new ministry settings)
- serving as a clearinghouse for coordinating and scheduling all youth events
- keeping the various groups for youth informed
- reporting to the church council
- planning special events or projects to include all youth related to the congregation's ministry (a youth-led worship service, for instance)
- supervising designated ongoing activities
- working with the committee on lay leadership selection, designating youth members to other official groups to fulfill disciplinary requirements (remember that youth may serve on all boards and committees except for trustees—the law requires trustees to be of majority age).

Fit Your Situation

It is important that your youth ministry leadership decides what kind of coordination you need. The council on youth ministry is one possibility, but there are many other ways of organizing. Another organization that can be particularly effective is forming "ministry coordination teams" in fellowship, service, worship, study, and outreach. Develop an organization designed to meet your own situation. (See *The United Methodist Youth Handbook* and other youth ministry resource books in the Resources for additional possibilities.)

The first tendency is to elect officers. This means that some win and some lose. Whenever someone really wants to help with planning or implementing ministries but is not elected to the council, everyone loses. Some ways of forming your council or teams *without holding elections* are by:

- **invitation.** Form a volunteer committee to invite the individuals who exhibit leadership traits to serve.
- **open invitation.** Invite anyone interested in providing leadership to a meeting to form a council.
- **application.** Persons can request the form themselves, or leaders can hand the form to the youth and adults they want to encourage to become more involved in leadership roles.
- **sign-up.** Develop a sign-up board or list to allow youth to volunteer.
- **discernment.** Meet as a total group, discuss the work to be done, read Scripture that gives guidance about maturity and wisdom, pray for God's guidance, encourage questions of clarification and exploration, spend time in silence, ask for insights gained (in this case about persons to serve as ministry leaders).

Getting a New Council Started

Gather interested youth and adults from the congregation to consider the same questions and issues found in "Getting Started." Your purpose is to determine realistic ministry goals. Spend time in prayer for God's direction in your task.

Decide what type of council structure would be the most effective in your circumstances (representative council, task forces, ministry coordination teams, elected, volunteer, selected, and so on).

Consider how you will handle issues of money, communication, accountability for program, calendar coordination, and other issues.

Spend time with the church staff and with lay leaders in the church discussing your proposed ministry goals and council structure. Listen closely to their suggestions and recommendations.

Develop job descriptions for proposed leadership positions.

When you are satisfied with your proposals, take them to the church council for approval. There will be a better partnership in youth ministry if the various councils and committees in your church fully understand each other's goals and structure.

After your council has been established, make it a point to evaluate its effectiveness regularly. Make modifications where necessary by adding short-term committees and task forces. More permanent modifications should be made each year before the selection of new leaders.

People Who Lead Youth Ministry

Youth lead youth. In his book, *Youth Ministry Handbook* (Abingdon Press, 1994, p. 21), Dr. Ed Trimmer says:

> Youth ministry is accomplished by youth. God's people, including youth, are involved with ministry in God's creation. Youth are no exception to this. They can minister to the church community, to the wider community, to the adults working with the youth ministry, and to youth themselves. Often, adults working with youth need to get out of the way and let them use the gifts God has given them. Youth, no less than adults, can be ministers in the New Testament sense of the word.

In youth ministry, you can provide youth with experiences that will help them become more Christ-like and find ways they can make a difference in the world.

Youth in leadership participate. In order for youth to lead others, they must first have followed. We learn much of what we know by experience. We learn much of our leadership skills from having been led by others.

By participating in youth ministry experiences, youth have the opportunity to grow spiritually and to experience fellowship with other youth and adults without having to be responsible for the activities. They can learn what it feels like to be a part of a Christian community without knowing how to create the community atmosphere. Once youth have experienced the growth, community, and fun of youth ministry, they are better prepared to learn leadership skills.

Identify youth leadership opportunities. "It shall be the duty of the pastor, the parent(s), guardian(s), sponsor(s), or godparent(s), the officers and teachers of the church school, the local church scouting coordinator, and all members of the congregation to provide training for the children of the Church throughout their childhood that will lead to a personal commitment to Jesus Christ as Lord and Savior, to an understanding of the Christian faith, and to an appreciation of the privileges and obligations of baptism and membership" (*Discipline,* ¶226.4).

- *Peer Leadership.* Youth have the ability to influence the way other youth think. As Christian leaders, they are expected to be examples among their peers.

- *Council on Youth Ministry or Ministry Team Member.* As a member of an elected council or as a member of a team, youth have the opportunity to guide the direction of the youth ministry in your church. Usually the older youth leaders tend to have more responsibility, while younger youth leaders have the opportunity to learn from the older youth. Each leader, older or younger, is expected to fulfill commitments he or she has made to the rest of the council, team, or youth group.

It is reasonable to expect the adult workers with youth to help youth get the training they need in order to be good leaders. Be sure to read the portions of these Guidelines that are focused on adults, too. The same skills that are recommended and expected of the adults are skills that will make youth better leaders of your group.

- *Member of a Board, Council, or Committee of Your Local Church.* The United Methodist Church recognizes youth as full and equal members of a local church. It also requires their presence as members of the planning and leadership groups within the church. The *Book of Discipline* requires that there be a youth (twelve to eighteen years old) on every committee in the church (except trustees), from the local congregation through all the general boards and agencies of The United Methodist Church.

Help your congregation seek to affirm and recognize the gifts of young people and invite them to be leaders. They are needed! Their energy, enthusiasm, and excitement bring newness to the wide variety of ministries that your church may explore and implement as expressions of their faith in Jesus Christ as Lord of their lives.

- *Do not invite youth into leadership just to "fill a position" or just do a job.* Offer an exciting invitation—an invitation for them to serve as leaders in your congregation and an invitation for them to grow in their faith, in their ability to share with others, and as disciples of Jesus Christ! Great invitations can lead to great experiences of life and love. Help them serve with joy!

Adult leaders are essential. Effective youth ministry does not exist without adult leaders. In fact, the most critical factor in an effective, long-term youth ministry is the ongoing presence of adults who are caring, confident, competent, and committed in their work with young people. The basic qualities needed to be an effective adult leader of youth are a vibrant and mature faith in and belief in Jesus Christ, as well as an appreciation for youth and what they can do. Other skills can be learned.

Sunday school classes require a group of committed adult teachers and workers who will encourage youth to explore the hard questions of the Christian faith. Effective Sunday school teachers attend training, use the resources provided by the local church (or search for excellent resources), and seek ways to continue their faith journey while they are serving as adult guides for youth.

For many adults in the local church, this commitment can seem overwhelming. Those persons in charge of recruiting volunteer teachers (a group consisting of youth and adults) should be specific about how teachers will be trained prior to their placement in the classroom. Encourage the formation of teaching teams or recruit persons to teach for a specific period of time. Provide a list of curriculum resource materials from which teachers may choose. (The youth section of the annual *Forecast* is particularly helpful. Copies are free and available from Cokesbury.)

UMY adult leaders carry a great responsibility. These adults often spend almost all of their "free" time with the youth and become the most important non-parent adults in the lives of youth.

For the adults who work with the UMY in general, and with the Fellowship groups in particular, it is a ministry of friendship. Youth need *adult friends who act like adults*. Youth need friends who will accept and advocate for them and challenge them to strive toward their potential. They need adults who will give them the benefit of adult wisdom and perspective. Adults can offer the love of Christ, which calls into question poor choices and inappropriate behavior without rejecting the youth. Such relationships in youth ministry may be the only chance a youth has to experience friendship with an adult. These friendships can be life-changing for youth, both assuring them that adolescence can be survived and even enjoyed, and also providing a model for Christian discipleship as an adult.

The responsibilities and expectations (by youth and by adults) of the adults who work with the UMY require a team approach. "Big Star" youth leaders set themselves up for exhaustion and early burnout. Generally, the one-adult youth group is limited to the amount of activity that one person is willing to supervise personally. When that person leaves, the ministry is in danger of falling apart.

Some Guidelines for Recruiting and Building Sunday School Teachers and the UMY Adult Team

- Look for persons who model a Christian lifestyle, who are able to give the advice of a parent without actually being the parent, and who can provide wisdom and perspective.
- Aim for as much variety as possible regarding age, marital status, parenthood, career.

- Ask the youth to list desirable qualities and then to suggest adults in the church who fit the criteria.
- Consider parents and guardians; some become very effective adult leaders. *Always* ask the young person before inviting his or her parent to become a leader.

Give people a realistic expectation of the job. People want to know:

- What am I being asked to do? How much time will it take? How long will it last?
- Who will be working with me? Do they have experience?
- What resources are available to help me? What training is available?
- Will this job put me on other committees in the church? What other meetings will I be expected to attend?
- How are the youth ministry activities financed, and how does that affect me?

Parents are, or can be, guides. A comprehensive approach to youth ministry sees parents as a pivotal factor in the faith development of youth; if parents lack active interest in the church, their children will most likely develop the same sense of indifference.

Being the parent of an adolescent is never easy. Often unpredictable, emotional, and stubborn, youth can frustrate their parents to the point that some parents "just let them do what they want." Congregations need to become caregivers, advocates, and educators to parents of the adolescents. Parents often feel wounded, deeply hurt in their attempts to reach out to the children they love. One of the first steps in developing parental involvement in youth ministry involves attending to the special needs of parents.

When supported and nurtured by a community of faith, parents can become active participants in ministry with and to youth, hosting youth events, providing transportation, chaperoning special events, leading discussion groups, and encouraging their sons and daughters to become active in the life of the local church.

Pastors and other church professionals are key people for effective youth ministry. Their enthusiastic support is crucial for communicating the importance of youth ministry to the entire congregation. They may also be the primary advocates to help the congregation recognize the gifts youth have to contribute. Pastors and church professionals should view themselves as a valued part of the youth ministry of the church. If they do, the youth will grow to accept them as such.

Benefits Pastors and Church Professionals Can Bring to the Youth Ministry Settings

- Church staff with training and experience in pastoral care can be very helpful in counseling youth and helping them develop their own skills as peer counselors.
- Pastors can encourage youth participation as leaders in worship.
- Church educators can lead a variety of encounters designed to teach youth the skills that will assist them in their faith journey. Confirmation, Bible groups, and short-term studies offer excellent opportunities for interaction with youth.
- Since the pastor is the chairperson of the committee on lay leadership, he or she can make sure there are youth members on all the congregation's official administrative groups.

Skill Building for Leaders of Youth Ministry

Effective youth ministry usually does not just happen. It requires leaders who have worked to improve their skills as spiritual leaders. Skill building does not often come quickly, nor is it ever complete. There is always something new to learn. It seems that just when a leader thinks that he or she really knows youth ministry, youth culture changes and the learning begins again. Training is particularly helpful in the following areas:

- theology and philosophy of youth ministry
- youth culture
- introduction to resources: finding them, adapting them, using them
- how to plan budgets, work camps, retreats, youth trips, parent training
- risk management
- relational, organizational, and spiritual guidance skills

The following lists of skill assets may be helpful as you seek to build leadership skills in youth ministry.

Relational Skills

Leaders (both adult and youth) are likely to be in several types of relationships—sometimes even several types with one person in the group.

Person-to-person. Adult and youth are both children of God. The only real difference is that one is older and has more experience than the other. Each has unique abilities and talents to contribute to the other and to the group. Each one needs to accept the other fully and with caring.

Adult-to-youth; youth-to-adult. The adult is not a youth, and the youth is not an adult. Each should act his or her own age, with no apologies and with no resentment toward the other. Furthermore, nothing is phonier than an adult trying to act like a teenager.

One-to-one. The fellowship setting is a group of individuals. A leader relates to a group best by relating to the individuals in it.

All relationship building in youth ministry requires several skills. The adults may need to develop these skills and help the youth to do the same.

Listen. For true communication, the speaker needs to feel that a leader is actively listening to what he or she has to say. When we truly listen, we use not only our ears but also our eyes, emotions, wisdom, and heart.

Respond. After listening comes response, for it is only through a response that the person is sure he or she has been heard. *Respond* is an active verb, and we can respond through encouragement, affirmation, and nonverbal gestures. This opens the door to new ideas and new relationships.

Speak. Sharing is opening and giving of oneself to someone else. The leader should never hold back appropriate sharing of ideas, concerns, and feelings with youth. However, this sharing should be done in the person-to-person mode and never as colonel-to-corporal.

Affirm. Youth need to be appreciated for who they are and what they do. Such affirmation comes in the form of both individual and group acknowledgments (congratulations), sharing information with others who in turn affirm the youth, and recognition through use of their leadership skills, special interests, and talents.

Encourage. Leaders can help youth grow by encouraging them to stretch their experiences and to try things they have never tried before that will deepen understandings, sharpen skills, and open doors into new worlds of discovery. The act of encouraging requires perception about where persons are in their development, sensitivity to their feelings and self-perceptions, and the willingness to be present with them in their ventures.

Empower. Empowering means to assist youth by helping them see, act out of, and grow through their own abilities. Adults can best empower when they stay in the wings and let the youth take center stage. Adults suggest, coach, encourage, congratulate, affirm, and support youth. When an adult empowers, he or she does everything possible to help the youth make decisions and plans that lead to successful conclusions.

Trust. Youth need to know they are trusted and respected by both their peers and the adults whom they respect. This is usually communicated by attitudes and actions rather than by words. One way to communicate trust is to take seriously the things youth say.

Adults do not have a greater responsibility to parents than they do to the youth. Do not betray the trust a youth might put in you by going to parents or to the pastor or to anyone else without permission of that youth. However, you do have a responsibility to the parents—they are now and have always been the primary source of help for the youth—and they love him or her. Your efforts to help a youth should include encouraging him or her to share the problem with the parents. If you feel you must reveal information to another person about a problem a youth has shared with you, be sure you have first told the youth of your intentions and your reasons.

Be approachable. In either serious matters or simple concerns, a leader can contribute to the emotional and spiritual growth of youth by being a person who is approachable and available.

Caution!

Be alert for problems beyond the limits of your counseling skills. When a problem calls for professional help, work with the appropriate persons to obtain that help for the youth. It is a good idea to check out the professional counselors in your area who work with youth so you will immediately know someone to whom you can refer youth if the need arises. Your pastor probably is trained in knowing how to find help in unusual circumstances.

Protect. The church and the youth ministry should be "safe sanctuaries" in which youth can grow in their relationship with God without fear of being harmed or abused—physically, emotionally, neglectfully, sexually, or ritually. Many churches have developed policies to screen individuals who work with children and youth and safety procedures to be followed during activities and outings.

Safeguarding Youth Ministry

Some common policies for prevention of abuse include:

- **Two-adult rule.** There is never just one adult present with youth.
- **Five-years-older rule.** Workers should be at least five years older than the people with whom they work and never younger than eighteen years old.
- **Sleeping arrangements.** Youth and adult never sleep in the same bed and preferably not in the same room on an outing.
- **Counseling.** One-on-one discussions are held only with the door open or in highly public places.
- **Windows rule.** There should be windows in all meeting room doors.
- **Screening procedures.** Adequate background checks are performed for individuals who work with children and youth.
- **Training about abuse.** Youth leaders must be aware that abuse can happen anywhere and know the facts about preventing it. Familiarity with the signs of abuse and knowledge of reporting procedures are essential for today's youth worker. A worker with youth must be prepared to tell if he or she suspects an abusive situation and to know the local laws about mandatory reporting.
- **Physical safety issues.** Youth workers should be conscious of safety concerns when leading activities and games. Proper equipment and adequate supervision of the activity should always be in place—one adult per eight to ten youth in normal situations.
- **Safe driving.** A youth worker who transports youth should be a safe driver and have proper credentials in the state of residence. The use of seat belts should always be enforced.
- **Insurance.** The church should be adequately insured for the scope of its youth activities.

For additional information, consult *Safe Sanctuaries for Youth: Reducing the Risk in Youth Ministries* (see Resources).

Organizational Skills

Organizational skills can make the difference between an average youth ministry and an exceptional one. Here are some functional skills needed for ministry with youth.

Planning. Good youth ministry requires sound planning and efficient implementation.

Gatekeeping. In order to ensure that all youth have the opportunity to participate in discussions and other activities, a leader may need to monitor a situation, making sure that some youth (or adults!) do not dominate while others are excluded. The leader can "open the gate" to those who are unsure and temporarily halt those who tend to take over.

Providing resources. Youth leaders often need help in discovering resources that will provide sound content for youth ministry, such as curriculum materials, books, videotapes, CD/DVDs and cassettes, movies, resource persons, games, and drama supplies. The adult leader is directly involved in providing the resources as well as suggesting sources to the youth. Learn to adapt resources to meet the abilities and interests of the group.

Selecting and scheduling. A group that is very active tends to bite off more than it can chew. A leader can advise the group about the number of items it can handle at one time. Scheduling events on a central calendar during planning sessions will be helpful in developing an effective youth ministry.

Training. Help inexperienced youth develop leadership abilities and participatory skills. Some areas for training include session planning, building agenda for meetings, leading sessions, working on committees, care giving, peer counseling, and asserting positive influence.

Advising. Adult workers are not meant to be passive observers, and advising is a part of their job. Although a youth group is primarily the property of its youth members, adults are there to provide knowledge, skills, and appropriate advice that will help the group members grow as Christian disciples and make the group a forum for examining Christian values.

Seeing the whole picture. In order to ensure a well-rounded ministry of service, worship, fellowship, outreach, and study, the youth group members must occasionally remind themselves of their reasons for being a group. The leaders are the key people in helping youth see the whole picture as they evaluate, discover strengths and weaknesses, dream, and plan. Mature abilities to observe, weigh options, keep track of plans, and evaluate in terms of variety, balance, and sound content are crucial to the group's well-being.

Requiring appropriate behavior. For any group to function responsibly, productively, and enjoyably, appropriate behavior is required. The most desirable discipline comes from within people; it is not superimposed from the outside. Discipline is not the responsibility of the adults alone, for they are advisors, not police officers.

Youth and adult leaders together, however, are often the ones who must enforce the rules and hold the youth accountable for unacceptable behavior. For times like these, be sure that the rules and the consequences have been made clear in advance. Act in a caring manner in all instances. Always explain to the youth involved why the rules or guidelines exist and why they must be adhered to. Take every instance seriously so as to uphold the expectations for the rest of the group. Also, allow for some mistakes to be made and be willing to practice forgiveness in the deepest sense. These will be opportunities for you to model God's grace.

Spiritual Guidance Skills

In order to be prepared to guide youth in the spiritual disciplines of Bible study, prayer, and meditation, both the youth and adult leaders should set aside some disciplined time each day to be alone with God. They should use this time to be more regular about the practice of these spiritual disciplines in their own lives. One cannot effectively guide others where one has not been.

It is recommended that leaders each find someone in their congregation or community whom they trust and respect as mature Christian disciples. Then they should ask these persons to be available for conversations and to act as guides during the time the leaders are seeking to guide the youth. Those who are not being spiritually nurtured soon deplete their resources to nurture others.

Many adult leaders who are new to youth ministry often are not very much more mature in their faith than the youth with whom they work. Some of these adults will awaken their spiritual growth while experiencing youth group activities. It is important for these adults to find spiritual growth groups with people their own age. That way they will be able to cope with issues facing them as adult Christians.

Leaders in youth ministry should develop their ability to use the traditional spiritual disciplines of prayer, Bible study, worship (especially the Lord's Supper), fasting, Christian conferencing (gathering together with other people to carefully seek God's will), and acts of mercy (helping other people).

Training Opportunities

One of the primary sources of training for youth ministry is *the youth themselves.* Adults who open themselves to these children of God will be amazed at how much they learn from them. A second source is *other adults who are experienced as adult youth leaders.*

Contact your district and conference coordinators or staff of youth ministry for a schedule of upcoming training events. If you have special training needs, let them know. These persons may be able to plan a training event to include your needs. District and conference coordinators and staff persons are usually available for *onsite training* in churches. If they cannot come, they can probably recommend other persons qualified to do such training.

The General Board of Discipleship sponsors *CONNECTION* (formerly FORUM)**,** national event for adult workers with youth offered once every four years. CONNECTION offers training, inspirational and informative speakers, meaningful worship, and networking with other United Methodist adults who work with youth. Contact your Conference Youth Coordinator, staff person, or CONNECTION, P.O. Box 340003, Nashville, TN 37203-0003, 615-340-7134.

Don't overlook training opportunities right in your own community. Hospitals and other social service agencies frequently conduct workshops and seminars pertaining to youth ministry. Call these agencies and get on their mailing lists.

Take advantage of events offered by other churches in your area. Join with them to bring in professionals that your church might not be able to afford by itself. Capitalize on the event later by creating an interdenominational support group of employed and volunteer youth leaders in your community that meets on a regular basis.

If you are planning to do your own training of new adult youth leaders, consider the following.

1. Invite these persons to sit in on several sessions in a Fellowship setting or another ministry with which they will work. This will help them begin to know the youth and to become familiar with the format of the ministry.
2. Provide resource materials (to be used in training as well as in the ministry) well in advance, so that persons can become familiar with the resources and refer to them easily in the training event itself.
3. Explain the steps in planning (long-term, short-term, session, and special event).
4. Explain the work of the planning groups in the leadership model you are using and the adult worker's relationship to these groups.
5. Provide time for the new leaders to ask questions and to react to experiences.
6. Let the new leaders know who is available to support them as they learn this new job.

Resources

People in your congregation and community. Members of your congregation and community are rich resources that can strengthen your youth ministry. These persons have much to offer by way of experience and skills in the whole scope of UMY activities.

Office of Youth Ministry, General Board of Discipleship, P.O. Box 340003, Nashville, TN 37203-0003. Telephone 615-340-7200. E-mail: shay@gbod.org, Web site: www.gbod.org/youth.

www.umc4youngpeople.org is a "gateway" Web site offering links to denominational Web sites related to youth ministry.

The Division on Ministries With Young People, P .O. Box 340003, Nashville, TN 37203-0003. Telephone 877-899- 2780, ext. 1780.
E-mail: youngpeople@gbod.org. The Division will oversee and advocate for ministries for and with youth and young adults, and administer the Youth Service Fund.

United Methodist curriculum resources: The United Methodist Publishing House (Forecast, Curric-U-Phone, www.ileadyouth.com). See the inside back cover.

Print Resources

The Bible. The heart of youth ministry resources is the Bible, which is an essential resource for whatever we do through the church.

The Book of Discipline of The United Methodist Church, 2004 (Nashville: The United Methodist Publishing House). The *Book of Discipline* is our book of covenant for The United Methodist Church. Available from Cokesbury.

Devo'Zine. (Upper Room) Devotional publication (by subscription) to help teenagers develop a lifetime pattern of prayer and spiritual reflection.

Faith-Forming Junior High Ministry: Beyond Pizza 101, by Drew A. Dyson (Nashville: Abingdon Press, 2003. ISBN 0-687-07539-4). A helpful, practical, and theological approach to junior high ministry.

Foundations: Shaping the Ministry of Christian Education in Your Congregation (Nashville: Discipleship Resources, 1993. ISBN 0-88177-123-6). The educational philosophy and approach for educational ministries based on "Our Theological Task," which appears in the *Book of Discipline*.

The Godbearing Life: The Art of Soul Tending for Youth Ministry, by Kenda C. Dean and Ron Foster (Nashville: Upper Room Books, 1998. ISBN 0-8358-0858-0). A working theology of youth ministry for United Methodist youth leaders.

Guidelines for Leading Your Congregation. (Nashville: Cokesbury, 2004.)

Job Descriptions & Leadership Development for Local Church Leaders, by Thomas R. Hawkins (Nashville: Discipleship Resources, 1997, 2001. ISBN 0-88177-344-1). A set of sheets describing the positions of all local church officers; includes a training manual for leadership development.

The Ministry of Christian Education and Formation: A Practical Guide for Your Congregation (Nashville: Discipleship Resources, 2003. ISBN 0-88177-395-6). Contains helpful information from how to plan budgets, to guidelines for meetings, to being a spiritual leader in the congregation.

Program Calendar shows special United Methodist dates and the Sunday lectionary passages as well as other helpful denominational information. Available from United Methodist Communications.

Safe Sanctuaries for Youth: Reducing the Risk of Abuse in Youth Ministries, by Joy Thornton Melton (Nashville: Discipleship Resources, 2003. ISBN 0-88177-404-9). Helps congregations develop policies to prevent abuse and provide safe environments for youth in their ministries settings.

The Structure and Organization of The United Methodist Church is a brief but very helpful description of the United Methodist Church system. Available from United Methodist Communications.

Together in Love: Covenant Discipleship with Youth, by David C. Sutherland (Nashville: Discipleship Resources, 1999. ISBN 0-88177-271-2). A guide on helping to start, maintain, and celebrate Covenant Discipleship groups in the local church setting.

The United Methodist Youth Handbook, by Michael Selleck (Nashville: Discipleship Resources, 1999. ISBN 0-88177-286-0). A guide for youth ministry leaders, youth and adult, as they build and enhance the ministries of a United Methodist congregation; helpful for volunteers and professionals, laity and clergy.